LOVE LETTERS

LOVE LETTERS

a collection of poems

TERRANCE P. ELMORE

Printed in the United States of America

First Printing, 2018

ISBN 978-0-9897328-7-1

Front and back cover image by Your World On Film

Truly In His Hands
307 N. Goose Creek
PO Box 1212
Goose Creek, SC 29445

For Nicole

.

"You're an inspiration in the most subtle and powerful way"
--- Beautiful

List of Experiences

List of Experiences

Introduction

My love for poetry began in elementary school. I can't remember my first poem but like most, if not all of us who's ever written poetry for the first time, it started with roses are red and ended with the word "you." Shortly after, I started getting poetry books from the library in addition to the fictional detective books I would normally check out. That's when I discovered Langston Hughes, who would later become my favorite poet.

My love for writing began with classroom assignments to write essays and short stories. It became something I looked forward to doing because it gave me a chance to create something from my thoughts. I loved the feeling of putting words together to paint a picture. I enjoyed people reading and liking something I created.

I decided to write poems about love because there are so many different interpretations but the beauty of love is always the same. This collection of poems is a small look into my interpretation of that beauty. It seems popular to say that love hurts or love is pain, but if you believe that, you haven't really experienced love. I believe that when real love is discovered and experienced, anything contrary to its beauty will be laid to rest.

Bloom

Flowers that bloom in the
romance of forever,
will always last in love's existence.

Breathe In

Inhaling the scent of perfume on
your skin, I start missing a place
I've never been to before.

I reflect back to memories we
haven't created. The perfume is
complimented by your skin.

It leads me places only my open
and unguarded heart can reach.
I've inhaled more than a scent. I
have inhaled you.

Her

From the first time I saw her I knew there was something about her. I didn't know what it was but I knew It was special and I had to protect it. I had to protect it like it was mine. Even before I knew I would make her mine and I would become hers.

Her smile is as beautiful as it is contagious. Her smile is the invitation to happiness. If her smile were a book you'd get lost in her pages. Her smile is soft in its presentation but powerful in its approach. Her smile is easy and never coached.

Her voice is the sound that awakens all that is great in you. From past triumphs to unreached victories. Her voice is what will always say, "I need you here with me." Her voice is the enhancement to everything I am and need to be. Her smile is what I look forward to when she becomes all she's meant to be.

Smile

Your smile fills the room
and enters my heart.

From this moment on
nothing will ever be the same.

What is this feeling
that has me enchanted with
curiosity?

What is this feeling
that has moved its way
to my thoughts?

What is this feeling
that I don't want to lose?

What is this feeling?

...it's been caused by your smile.

At First Sight

Love at first sight is possible when there's an anticipation of love. When there's an expectancy and readiness for love.

The idea is carried and nurtured with the promise of love. Protected with loves wisdom and compassion. We begin to encounter the timelessness of love once we acknowledge its presence.

Naked

I want to undress
your
mind
and
expose your thoughts—

so I can cover your heart and
protect your feelings.

Looking at You

Looking at you I see my future.

The experiences that are ahead of
us...
are how you'll share the view.

When I look at you
I see a part of me I've never seen
before.

A part of me that wants real love
more and more.

She Saw Love

She loves him because she was able to see love in him. She saw the qualities of love that were infused with the endlessness of love.

He would be the calming wind to chaos that laid rest in her heart from many disappoints. From self-disappointments to selfless love that was given but never reciprocated.

She saw how her belief in the existence of love was what the love he had inside was starving for, and it would die without her. She loves him because he is able to show her more love than she was allowed to see.

Wants and Needs

I want you here right now
because I need you next to me.

I want you to talk to me because I
need to hear your voice.

I want you to open your arms
because I need to hug you.

I need to tell you something
so I want to be honest with you.

I need you to know I love you
so I want to show you.

I need you in my life forever so I
say I do.

Full

With my words…
I will build you up and encourage
you.

With my love…
I will protect you and support you.

Your strength and courage are the
foundation of fulfillment.

Endless Beginnings

The destination only has room for
what's new
and created between the two.

> Old things left behind
> along the way. New
> memories created for a
> new day.

Growth and progress are easiest
when carrying less. Closed
chapters not to be given a second
look. This is the beginning of an
endless and meaningful book.

Aim

He aims for the universe
so that he can give her the world.

She aims for forever
so that they can share a lifetime.

Together they aim for perfection
so that every experience along the
way creates indestructible passion.

Authenticity

We can be much more...
than two people attracted to each
other at first sight.

We can be much more...
than two people who enjoy each
other's conversation and talk all
night.

We can be much more...
than two people who respect each
other's dissimilarity.

We can be much more...
than two people who talk about
their problems to gain clarity.

We can be much more...
than just two people in love.

We WILL be the example of all
that's possible in the authenticity
of love.

Search

If you search, you will find me.
If you search, you will see me.
If you search, you will talk to me.
If you search, you will learn me.
If you search, you will hold me.
If you search, you will feel me.
If you search, you will complete
me.
If you search, I will love you
forever.

If I search...
I will discover you were here the
entire time.

Home

Pack a few things because there
won't be a return.

Bring a few memories…

like the first time we met
and the first time we kissed.
or that one time I embarrassed
myself trying to look cool.

> Ok maybe it was more
> than once.

Don't forget the experiences that
we learned from and the ones that
helped us grow.

Bring your dreams and together
we'll make them goals.

Oh yeah and the plans for our
future together because we'll need
those to get where we are going.

Bring all of these things with you
because you have a new home.
My heart.

To Love You

I'm going to love you with parts of my heart that have never felt love before.

I'm going to love you with genuineness and kindness that grows each day more and more.

I'm going to love like it's new because real love never existed before I met you.

I'm going to love you the way you deserve to be loved. The way love is supposed to be. The kind of love you'll feel as your sitting next to me.

I'm going to love you with the desire to learn how to love you the way you need to be loved. The desire to love better each day. To love you stronger each day.

I'm going to love you the right way because there is no other way. I'm going to love you without the limits that fear and uncertainty bring.

I'm going to love you the way love is supposed to be.

Your Heart

I'll protect your heart with the love
that lives in my heart.

The love that lives in my heart is
intense like fire. A fire that only
burns for you.

I'll protect your heart with strength
that's saturated with the power of
love.

I'll protect your heart with passion
because it's my desire to protect
your heart and love you always.

My All

With every touch.
With every hug.
With every kiss.
With every opportunity.

With all my heart.
With all my effort.
With all my attention.
With all my desire.

My love is growing and will never
die.

I Love You

I love you.
I am in love with you.
> My love belongs to you.
> My love is you.

I love how you love me.
I love how I love you.
I love who you are.
I love who you will be.
> I love who I am and will
> be because of you.

I love our conversations.
I love our dreams.
I love how our dreams became
goals. I love our achievements.
> I love our disappointments
> that made us stronger. I
> love that we grow closer
> together and never further
> apart.

I love making plans with you.
I love spending time with you.
> I love that you're the piece
> to the puzzle my life was
> missing.

I love your determination. I love
your dedication.
> I love you.

One Day

Today is what became of one day.

What started as a thought…
developed into a need fueled by
desire.

The desire to experience
something real and new.

The desire to express and give.
The desire to create and build.
The desire to be better than the
day before.

A desire to plan for the future.
Our future.

Real Love

I never knew a love like this...
Felt so deeply.
Even from the smallest kiss.

I never knew a love so sweet...
Our hearts connect to form one
beat.

I never knew a love so true...
Then again I've never had a love
like you.

I never knew love...

Because I never had love.

Free

Free to laugh. Free to smile.
Free to remain here for longer
than just a while.

Free to dream. Free to make goals.
Free to be made whole.

Free from sadness. Free to cry.
Free to let overwhelming joy and
happiness be why.

Free to be. Free to become. Free
to accept you've found the one.

Free to care. Free to love. Free to
thank God for the blessings that
come from above.

Touched

An encounter with you.
A moment with you.
A thought of you.
A yearning for you.
A longing for you.
A want for you.
A desire for you.
A love for only you...

Once I've touched you.

Sweet

Sweet as the taste of flavors
enjoyed for the first time.

Sweet as the thoughts of love and
happiness that flow through my
mind.

A sweetness like no other,
as it is
the origin
of all good things to come.

A sweetness that will always
move
to the beat
of
love's undying drum.

Inspiration

The SPARK that sets you on the
path to life's purpose and meaning.
The embrace beauty's nature. Pure
in form and spirit.

The first time your eyes meet
theirs.
The connection between what
could be and what will be.

It's the reassurance of knowing
impossible no longer exists.
   I can do this.
   I will do this.
   I have accomplished it.

Words of encouragement. Words
of admiration…

They reach and release the deepest
parts of your creativity.
      Inspiration.

Sensuality

It's the touch that caresses without hands. It's the gentle kiss on the heart from the lyrics of love.

The embrace made by conversation that stimulates the creativity hidden deep within.

The attractiveness of intelligence. The endless climax of ambition and authenticity.

It's the quintessential meaning of sensuality.

Happiness

It grabs you close and holds you tight. But releases you from all binds and sets you free. It turns heartache into accomplishment. It turns what ifs into lasting memories.

Its true nature can only be found from within ourselves, but many still search for it in others. It may not last forever, but because of it your favorite memories will last forever.

It comes at a time when you least expect it. At a time where you know it's missing but you aren't looking for it. It's when you realize everything you've gone through was worth it.

Appreciated

I really love you.
Thank you for all that you do.
Appreciated.

Expressions

A gentle touch from one hand to
another.

The subtle glance---
even when you're within arm's
reach.

The look back after you've said
your goodnights and parted ways.

The extra moments spent on the
embrace of a familiar hug.

The unexpected I love you's
throughout the day. Those random
"I didn't want anything, just
wanted to hear your voice" phone
calls.

Soft kisses on the forehead when
you're sleeping in their arms.

I love you and I'll always be here.

If

If
I
could
relive this moment…

      it would be forever.

If
I
could
change this moment…

      it would remain the same.

If
I
could
replace you in this moment…

      we would endure.

More

I want more of this feeling.
>   It's like nothing I've ever
>   felt before. Its taste is
>   sweet. Its touch is
>   complete.

I want more of you.
>   Tell me what your goals
>   are and what you aspire to
>   be. Show me who you
>   really are. Let go and be
>   free.

I want more of us.

Faded

The fade of time lives in its existence.
The immortality of time lives within memories.
The fade of beauty is held in the hands of time.

The immortality of beauty lives within the heart.
True beauty lives in the memories of the heart.

Hugs

A hold that's much more than an embrace.

Much more than your arms around my neck and mine around your waist.

Much more than how I greet you.

The way you feel love—

Let me teach you.

Kiss

Subtle in its delivery.
Uncategorized in its intent. A
message in its action.

Lips to cheek.

Delivered with a presence of
intimacy. Intended with a purpose.
A meaningful action.

Lips to forehead.

Deliberately delivered. Passionate
in purpose. An action of intimacy.

Lips to lips.

Midnight

Hey…
Are you asleep?
It sounds like you're asleep.
     Guess what…

 I love you.

Whisper

Soft words that are only meant to
be heard by you.
Spoken from the heart with
nothing new.

Promises made that will be kept...

Telling how proud of you I am
and how much I love you—
as you slept.

I want to tell the world how I feel.
So I whisper the words to you
because you are my world
and our love is real.

She

She wakes me up in the morning
with a soft whisper and a kiss on
the cheek...
> "good morning,"
> she says...
> "it's time to start your day."

It's so sweet and mellow that now
I'm contemplating.
> Should I get up?
> Or just chill and lay?

Ahhh I guess I'll get up.

I go hit the shower and she's there
waiting but she's talking louder.
Not disrespectfully but to get me
hype. Now I got this soap and
water on my body and I'm feeling
right.

Some mornings I might not take
her with me but most mornings
she's right here. Helping me get
through this traffic and telling me
she will always care.

Whatever the day brings I can
count on her voice to take me to
another place, change my mood,
or keep me in a mood that makes
me want to sing.

She can be sassy with without
hesitation or she can sing words of
love and dedication. She can get
me hyped and ready for the gym
or she can sooth me into a place of
meditation.

She has been known to put a time
stamp on things of the past. But
we'll only talk about the good
memories…you know the things
we want to last.

This is she
and she
will always be.

Weekends

When the week gets busy,
it's you I long for.

The last time I was with you and
the next time we'll be together are
the thoughts that cross my mind.

When the week gets tiresome,
it's you that will make the
difference.
> Whether naps in the
> middle
> of the day or a short
> getaway.

When the week is difficult,
it's your easy ways that I need.
> Relaxation
> and comfort—
> is all you require.

During the week it's early
breakfast but with you it's a late
brunch or sometimes lunch starts
the day.

During the week it's all about the 9
to 5 but with you only Sunday
morning worship is all that's
guaranteed.

When we part ways it's never
goodbye, it's always see you soon.

Rain

Outside of my window is the
sound of your voice.

I
love
to hear you speak.

Looking out the window.

I
love
to watch you dance.

I'm relaxed.
In love with your presence.

Sunset

Late afternoon walks with
conversation.
Late afternoon walks with a gentle
breeze.

Late afternoon walks with you.

Late afternoon walks looking at
the sunset.

Laughter

Sometimes it starts with a smile…

A happy uninterrupted moment.
Triggered by a thought or
sometimes nothing at all. A
connection between long lost
friends that never dies.

Sometimes it starts as a light
introduction of what's to come.

A happy uninterrupted moment. A
connection between siblings
foreign to their parents.

Sometimes it starts right in the
middle.

A happy uninterrupted moment. An
inside joke between two people in
love.

A happy uninterrupted lifetime.
Laughter

We

TWO hearts on a single path to balance.

TWO hearts that pump purpose and fulfillment.

TWO hearts that are strengthened by kindness and understanding.

TWO hearts beating with preparation and expectancy.

TWO hearts with a common interest.

TWO hearts in the oneness of love.

TWO hearts in the wholeness of love.

TWO hearts existing in the simplicity of love.

Proud

I'm proud
of who you are.

I'm proud
of who you're not.

I'm proud
of who you were
because it's made you who you are
and who you'll become.

I'm proud
of how you inspire others and how
you inspire me.

I'm proud
of your strengths.

I'm proud
of your weaknesses.

I'm proud of all these things
because
I'm proud of your character.

Pictures

A father holding his child for the first time. Excited and proud about their future.

The kiss from a grandmother on juniors first birthday. Remembering when his mother was that age.

The uncertainty of the first day of school. Smiling big because you're wearing a new outfit.

Standing with cousins who are more like siblings. Whose pose is the coolest and who can make the weirdest faces.

Prom night dressed to impress. Hoping you look as good as you think you do when the camera man says cheese.

Graduation time is finally here. Standing with your diploma you feel so proud.

She said yes. Showing of the ring smiling and happy.

Your first child is born. Pictures.

She Likes Me

I think she likes me…
but I'm not sure.

I mean she laughs at my jokes and
smiles…
but she could just be trying to be
nice.

Once she told me she likes my
haircut, but I don't get a haircut
everyday so I don't think that
means she likes me.

She always tells me I'm a nice guy,
but she's cool and cool people say
things like that.

One day she asked me why I
haven't asked her out on a date
yet.
I think I've got my answer.

Hello

Let me say hello
Never let me say goodbye
Just see you later

Morning

Thank God for seeing another day.
Good morning.
How did you sleep?
I hope you dreamt of me.

      I'll be
      thinking of you
      throughout the day.

Good morning.

Enjoy your day.

Conversations

Intrigued by topics deeper than
what's your favorite color.
More like do you see yourself in
the future as a mother?

Paying attention to the words you
use and the tone in your voice.
Making sure this conversation isn't
forced but filled with smiles and
laughter because your choice.

More than just talking...
communicating with each other
and expressing how we feel.

It's so refreshing to have a
conversation with someone that's
genuine and real.

Conversations that turn dreams
into goals. Conversations that for
great things ahead, it's the mold.
Conversations.

Good Night

As the end of the night draws
near...

I'm reflecting back on the evening
we've just experienced together.

I'm reflecting on how tomorrow
morning when I open my eyes this
very moment will be on my mind.

I'm reflecting to that moment
when I asked, "can I take you out
to dinner" and you said, "yes".

I'm reflecting back to the songs I
was singing when I was in the
shower getting ready.

I'm reflecting back to the
conversations I anticipated us
having as I practiced and prepped.
I'm reflecting back to when I
finally got dressed and the
nervousness set in. "Keep your
cool" is what I kept telling myself.

I'm reflecting back to the car ride
on the way to pick you up. Trying
to get the right music together.
Something sexy but not suggestive.
Something smooth but not
seductive...or should we ride in
silence?

I'm reflecting back to when I rang
the doorbell. You answered the
door with the most beautiful smile
my eyes have ever seen.

I'm reflecting back to how the
evening had none of the
conversations I had rehearsed.

And it's cool because the
conversations we did have were
better than I could've imagined.

Now we're at this moment.

I kiss you—

on your forehead and say good
night.

I Miss You

Last night
you met me in my dreams.

Last night
in my dreams
you were there.

The morning came and I opened
my eyes but you weren't near.
When I opened my eyes I thought
you were with me but you weren't.

You were with me in my dreams
but now I'm awake.

In my dreams you were there but
I'm awake and you're not here.

I miss you.

Get Back to You

Phone conversations, texts, or
FaceTime. There's only one thing
that's on my mind.

I must get back to you.

I love you.
I am thinking about you.
I miss you.

I have to get back to you.

Thinking at Night

At night I think about you...

I think about you throughout the day, but it's the night time, when the loudest part of silence is without the sound of your voice.

When the stars are kissing the sky, I am thinking about kissing you.

The light shines down from a distant moon like the presence felt from a distant love. At night I'm thinking about you.

On My Way Home

I've been thinking about you all
day. I can't wait to see you, so I'm
on my way.

Can't wait to hug and kiss you.
Can't wait to show you how much
I miss you.

How peaceful it is to hear your
voice face to face. You will always
feel protected whenever my arms
are wrapped around your waist.

I'll be here forever.
Not just right now.
If you give me a lifetime—
I'll show you how.

Infallible

True love is
and
will forever be.

It can never be what we try to
force it to be.

It exposes who we really are, for
anything counterfeit cannot exist
in its presence.

It makes us who we are.

Striving to be part of its perfect
balance.

Untitled

Without substance…

words
      are
only
      arranged
letters.

Existing unbalanced and fragile.

Meaning is substance.
Intent is substance.
Kept promises are substance.

      Balanced and strong.

Words

Words with substance…

become more than just arranged letters.

Words with meaning are vessels filled with hope and promise.

Words with content are structured with the stability of joy.

Words with a destination travel with ambition.

Words filled with affection, warmth, and love are words filled with love.

Love's Fragrance

The air is filled with its familiar but undiscovered fragrance.

> Does this fragrance
> exist in memory?
> Or is its familiarity
> only within its
> understanding?

The fragrance of promises kept. The fragrance of dreams becoming reality

A fragrance that soothes the soul once it touches your nose. A fragrance that awakens your purpose when it touches your skin.

I think I like it and I want it to linger on forever...

What is this fragrance and why am I smelling it for the first time?

The answer lies with in my heart as this is the fragrance of love.

Slow Dance

I've been watching you all night
and you've been watching me.
Now the dance floor is open and
the lights are low. Take my hand
and lead me to the dance floor,
turn and meet me with those eyes.

My hands around your waist.
Your arms around my neck.—
I'm lost in your eyes.

The dance floor is full but at this
moment there's only us. We begin
to move to a rhythm. In sync with
the music but the rhythm we're
moving to is a different song. The
rhythm is happiness and joy. A
song of love and fullness.

As we dance,
we are in harmony.

As we dance,
we are wrapped in each other.

As we dance,
we are posed with strength.

As we dance,
we are one.

As we dance we are love.

Time

It wasn't used wisely so it was no longer about enjoying the moments. It became the measurement between the moments.

It was no longer about the memories. It became record of what happened.

It's was longer not enough.
It became too long.

But then it was renewed and restored to become all it was meant to be.

Be

Live in the moment
and don't take one second for
granted.

Life is a blessing,
so be purposeful and true.

Share more than pictures but also
the experiences that get you there.

Inspire others to be who they were
created to be.

Never give up and let kindness be
your voice.

You are here for a reason.

Thank you God for this gift and
opportunity.

Thank you for reading Love
Letters.

40689387R00077

Made in the USA
Middletown, DE
29 March 2019